PORT

*Rhoc*

**Steck-Vaughn Company**

|  |  |
|---|---|
| **Executive Editor** | Diane Sharpe |
| **Senior Editor** | Martin S. Saiewitz |
| **Design Manager** | Pamela Heaney |
| **Photo Editor** | Margie Foster |
| **Electronic Cover Graphics** | Alan Klemp |

**Proof Positive/Farrowlyne Associates, Inc.**
Program Editorial, Revision Development, Design, and Production

**Consultant:** Becky Bovell, Assistant Director of Tourism

Published by Raintree Steck-Vaughn Publishers, an imprint of Steck-Vaughn Company.

A Turner Educational Services, Inc. book. Based on the Portrait of America television series by R. E. (Ted) Turner.

**Cover Photo:** New Harbor Block Island by © Superstock.

**Library of Congress Cataloging-in-Publication Data**

Thompson, Kathleen.
    Rhode Island / Kathleen Thompson.
       p.   cm. — (Portrait of America)
    "Based on the Portrait of America television series"—T.p. verso.
    "A Turner book."
    Includes index.
    ISBN 0-8114-7385-6 (library binding).—ISBN 0-8114-7466-6 (softcover)
    1. Rhode Island—Juvenile literature. I. Title. II. Series:
Thompson, Kathleen. Portrait of America.
F79.3.T48  1996
974.5—dc20

                                  95-44413
                                     CIP
                                     AC

Printed and Bound in the United States of America

2 3 4 5 6 7 8 9 10 WZ 02 01 99 98

**Acknowledgments**
The publishers wish to thank the following for permission to reproduce photographs:
Pp. 7, 8 © Jim McElholm; pp. 10, 11, 12 The Rhode Island Historical Society; p. 14 © Peter Gridley/FPG; p. 15 Slater Mill Historic Site; pp. 16, 17, 18 The Rhode Island Historical Society; p. 19 (left) © Clyde H. Smith/Tony Stone Images, (right) © Jim McElholm; pp. 20, 21 The Rhode Island Historical Society; p. 22 © Richard Laird/FPG; p. 24 The Monet Group; p. 25 U.S. Department of Defense/Department of the Navy; p. 26 (top) © C. A. Browning/Rhode Island Department of Economic Development, (middle) © Jim McElholm, (bottom) © Robert H. I. Goddard; p. 27 (top) © Jim McElholm, (bottom) Rhode Island Tourism Division; p. 29 (top) Diane Worthen, (bottom) © Jim McElholm/Greater Providence Convention & Visitors Bureau; p. 30 © Richard Laird/FPG; p. 32 © Michael Reagan; p. 34 (top) © Amour Photography/Beechwood Mansion, (bottom) © Vietry Photography/Beechwood Mansion; p. 35 Greater Providence Convention & Visitors Bureau; p. 36 Courtesy Matthew Tracy; p. 37 (top) © Robert & Sue Newman, (bottom) Carousel Park Commission; pp. 38, 39, 40, 41 © Jim McElholm; p. 42 © Peter Gridley/FPG; p. 44 © Clyde H. Smith/Tony Stone Images; p. 46 One Mile Up; p. 47 (left) One Mile Up, (center, right) Rhode Island Department of Economic Development.

STECK-VAUGHN

PORTRAIT OF AMERICA

# Rhode Island

Kathleen Thompson

A Turner Book

RAINTREE
STECK-VAUGHN
PUBLISHERS
The Steck-Vaughn Company

*Austin, Texas*

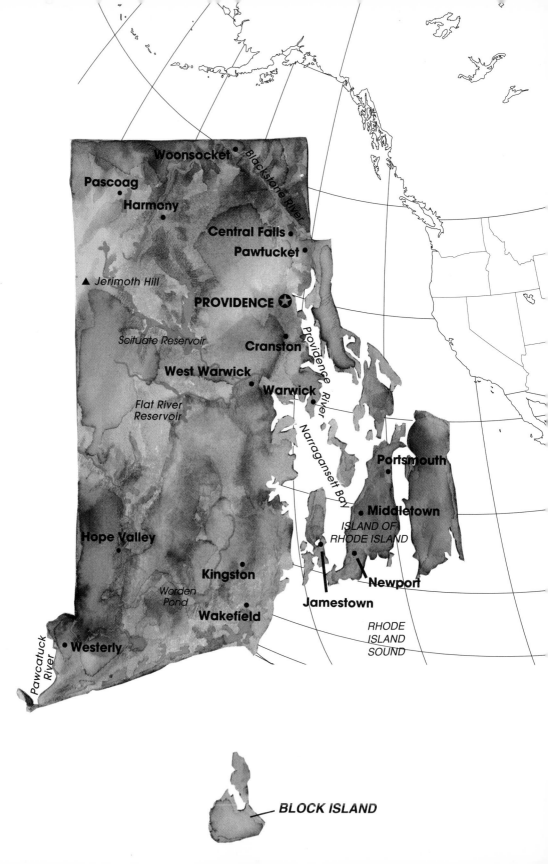

**Rhode Island**

Woonsocket

Pascoag

Harmony

Central Falls

Pawtucket

*Blackstone River*

▲ *Jerimoth Hill*

PROVIDENCE ✪

*Scituate Reservoir*

Cranston

West Warwick

Warwick

*Providence River*

*Flat River Reservoir*

Portsmouth

*Narragansett Bay*

Middletown

*ISLAND OF RHODE ISLAND*

Hope Valley

Kingston

Newport

*Worden Pond*

Jamestown

Wakefield

*RHODE ISLAND SOUND*

*Pawcatuck River*

• Westerly

**BLOCK ISLAND**

# Contents

# Introduction

Rhode Island is the smallest state in the United States, but its accomplishments in history and industry are large. Founded as a place for religious and political freedom, Rhode Island was the first state to declare its independence from Great Britain in 1776. The people of Rhode Island have always been inventive and hardworking. They began the American textile industry and the nation's jewelry industry. They've also rebuilt and restored the original masterworks of Rhode Island architecture. Rhode Island is made up of the mainland and 36 islands. What links the people of these islands together does not show; it is leadership, industriousness, and pride in Rhode Island accomplishments.

Rhode Island contains many historic buildings. This house in Newport was built around 1740.

# Rhode Island

Narragansett Bay,  colonial buildings,  Providence

# The Rhode Island Way

By the time European explorers arrived in the 1500s, about ten thousand Native Americans lived in the Rhode Island area. The most numerous of these were the Narragansett, who made up about half of the people living there. Four other groups occupied land in the region. These were the Wampanoag, the Niantic, the Nipmuc, and the Pequot.

All these peoples belonged to the Algonquian family of Native Americans. Various Algonquian peoples lived throughout much of what is now the eastern United States and eastern Canada. For the most part, they lived peacefully. But there were occasional battles between the Narragansett and the Wampanoag, who lived on the western shores of Narragansett Bay, in the extreme eastern area of Rhode Island.

The Algonquian peoples lived in villages, which they built near bodies of water. Their round-topped dwellings, called wigwams by European settlers, were made of a framework of wooden poles covered with skins, tree bark, or mats woven from reeds. The

The armory of the Artillery Company of Newport is now a military museum. It was built in 1835 and contains military memorabilia from over one hundred countries.

This 1925 photo shows a group of Narragansett in traditional clothing, in front of the Old Stone Church in Charlestown.

Algonquians grew corn, beans, and squash, and gathered roots and berries. They hunted deer and birds, and fished with nets, spears, and bone hooks. The Algonquian people had developed a system of government in which legal and spiritual disputes were resolved by village leaders.

In 1524 an Italian explorer named Giovanni da Verrazano explored the region. He thought present-day Block Island, which is about 12 miles south of the mainland, resembled the Greek island of Rhodes. Verrazano wrote a very favorable account of the surrounding area, including the island. He called the area Rhode Island. In 1614 a Dutch navigator named Adriaen Block sailed into Rhode Island waters. He named Block Island after himself.

The story of Rhode Island's first European settlement begins in present-day Massachusetts. In 1628 a religious group called the Puritans established the Massachusetts Bay Colony, about fifty miles north of

Plymouth. The Puritans left England because they disagreed with some of the practices of the Church of England. They were called Puritans because they wanted to practice a "purified" form of religion. Some settled in Boston, and others founded a colony in Salem. The Puritans lived according to strict rules, which were enforced by Governor John Winthrop.

A young preacher named Roger Williams arrived in Boston in 1631. Williams believed in religious freedom, and he felt that everyone should worship God in his or her own way. He expressed the opinion that the rules of the church should be separate from government laws. In addition Williams believed that colonists should pay the Native Americans for their land. His beliefs angered the Puritan colonists, and Williams was arrested several times for expressing "dangerous opinions."

In January 1636 Governor Winthrop ordered Williams back to England. Leaving his wife and two daughters, Williams fled south instead. He spent the winter with the friendly Wampanoag on the east side of Narragansett Bay. Others from the Massachusetts colony who shared his beliefs joined him there. Then, in June 1636, Williams bought some land from the Narragansett and founded a town at the north end of Narragansett Bay. He named it Providence, because he believed that God's providence, or watchful care, had kept them safe.

Williams sent for his family and spread the word that his new colony welcomed anyone who wanted religious and political freedom. Soon a steady stream of people from Massachusetts came to Rhode Island. Some settled in Providence. Others founded the towns

Roger Williams, the free-thinking founder of Rhode Island, is shown on his journey through the harsh New England winter in this nineteenth-century painting.

of Portsmouth, Newport, and Warwick, all on the shores of Narragansett Bay.

However, not everyone who came was interested in religious freedom. Some people were more interested in escaping from the strict rules of the Puritan colonies. In time Rhode Island gained a reputation as a place for troublemakers. It began to be known as "Rogues' Island."

In 1644 Roger Williams received an official charter for the colony from the English Parliament. The charter officially separated the Rhode Island Colony from Massachusetts. It took three years for the new colony's four towns to agree on a single form of government. Finally, they agreed that each town would retain some independence. Even then there were disagreements between the towns. A second charter was issued in 1663, and it remained the basis of government for 180 years.

For nearly forty years, Rhode Islanders lived in peace with the Native Americans, partly because they paid for the land they settled on. Trouble came from the area of the Massachusetts colonies, when Native Americans there began to resist further takeovers of their land. In 1675 a Wampanoag chief named Metacomet, whom the colonists called King Philip, began attacking colonial settlements in Massachusetts. He persuaded warriors from many other Native American groups to aid in the

This lithograph shows the Wampanoag chief Metacomet.

fight. Even some of the Narragansett joined in. At first most of the fighting was directed against Massachusetts settlers. However, in December 1675, a militia from Massachusetts and Connecticut defeated Native American warriors in a battle called the Great Swamp Fight. It took place near what is now Kingston, in southern Rhode Island. After the battle the colonists burned the Native American village and killed everyone there. About 700 Native American men, women, and children were slain.

After the Great Swamp Fight, Native Americans began to attack Rhode Island settlements. All the mainland settlements were damaged, and about half of Providence was burned to the ground. Most of the colonists took refuge on the offshore islands. In 1676 Metacomet was killed near Mount Hope, now Bristol. Two years later the war was over.

Part of Rhode Island's economy was based on trade with the West Indies. Merchants sold horses, salt, fish, wood, and other products. Later, Rhode Island merchants entered the "triangular trade." They sent rum to Africa, where it was traded for slaves. They took the slaves to the West Indies and traded them for molasses. Then they brought the molasses back to Rhode Island, where it was made into more rum.

In 1764 the British Parliament passed the Sugar Act, which charged a tax on the import of foreign molasses, sugar, wine, and other goods. These taxes interfered with the triangular trade and angered colonists. In protest Rhode Islanders began smuggling the goods into the colony without paying the tax. Colonial unrest turned to violence in 1769 when Rhode

This statue in Newport's King's Park honors the Comte de Rochambeau. General Rochambeau commanded French troops sent to aid the American colonies during the Revolutionary War.

Islanders burned the British ship *Liberty* at Newport. In 1772 another British ship, *Gaspee*, chased a Rhode Island trade ship in Narragansett Bay. The *Gaspee* ran aground in the night, and the people of Providence boarded the ship, shot and wounded its captain, and burned it. These were some of the first acts of violence leading up to the Revolutionary War.

During the Revolutionary War, which began in 1775, Newport was taken over by the British, and there were raids on other settlements. Hundreds of Rhode Islanders fought against the British. On May 4, 1776, Rhode Island was the first colony to declare its independence from Great Britain. At the end of the Revolutionary War in 1783, the colonies became the United States of America.

Delaware and Rhode Island were the smallest of the 13 original states. Delaware, because of its size, felt the need for protection by the other states. It was the first state to approve the new Constitution. Rhode Island held out until May 29, 1790. Its people wanted to be sure their individual rights would be protected. They did not approve the Constitution until they were certain that the ten amendments called the Bill of Rights would be added to the Constitution.

In the 1790s Rhode Island began to rely less on trade. The colony turned to manufacturing—especially textiles. Moses Brown, a rich and powerful Providence citizen, wanted to build mills like those he had seen in Great Britain. These mills had water-powered machines that could spin cotton into thread. Rhode Island had many swift streams to supply the power. The problem was getting the plans to build these machines. The British wanted no competition for their textile industry. The construction of their textile machines was so secret that people who had worked with them were not allowed to leave the country! However, a man named Samuel Slater studied how the machines were made and sneaked out of Great Britain disguised as a farmer. He came to Pawtucket and in 1790 built a spinning machine from memory for Brown.

Within ten years many other textile mills were built on the banks of Rhode Island rivers. In 1794 Providence resident Nehemiah Dodge invented metal plating, which was a way to apply precious metals as a covering for cheap metals. Rhode Island became the center in America for the manufacture of jewelry and silver-plated eating utensils. In 1810 David Wilkinson

Samuel Slater's mill in Pawtucket was the first successful water-powered cotton mill in the United States.

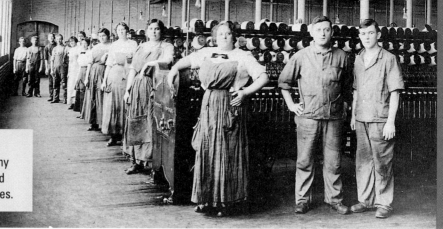

These workers at the Royal Weaving Company in the late 1800s worked long hours for low wages.

built a mill that used water power to make metal tools and equipment. Along with fishing and whaling, these industries brought wealth to Rhode Islanders.

When hardship struck in other countries, people sailed to the United States in search of a better life. Many of these people were poor and undereducated. They had little choice but to work in the mills for low wages. Working conditions were terrible in the mills. Whole families, including children, had to work long hours just to make enough money to live.

As the cities filled up, it became clear that Rhode Island's laws were out of date. The charter of 1663 was still the foundation of state law. The law limited the right to vote to male landowners and their oldest sons. By 1840, Rhode Island had more than one hundred thousand residents. Many of Providence's men could not vote because they did not own property. Women were not allowed to vote at all. Rural towns with far fewer residents, but more male landowners, regularly outvoted Providence in the state legislature.

In 1842 a man named Thomas Dorr tried to form a new government to protest this situation. He and his followers held the People's Party Convention, in which they created a new state constitution that gave voting rights to all adult males. Dorr's People's party then held its own statewide election. Dorr was elected governor. Naturally the official state government refused to recognize these illegal actions. State troops arrested Dorr and the leaders of his party and convicted them of treason. However, Dorr's rebellion showed the state government how upset many people were with the out-of-date laws. In 1842 Rhode Island adopted a new constitution that gave more men the right to vote.

From 1861 to 1865, Rhode Island fought on the Union side during the Civil War. More than 24,000 Rhode Islanders served in the Civil War. After the war, industry continued to grow. By 1900 the population of Rhode Island had more than doubled since the 1860s.

Rhode Island's economy ran into trouble in the 1920s. Textile companies began moving their mills to southern states. Factory owners could save money by operating where the cotton was grown. Also, many people in the southern states were unemployed and willing to work for low wages. By the 1930s, when the Great Depression was affecting the country, Rhode Island's main industry had continued to decline. Working conditions in the remaining factories continued to be very bad. Attempts to organize workers into labor unions failed because many workers were afraid they would lose their jobs.

The Second Rhode Island Regiment fought in the Civil War under General Ambrose Burnside. This photo shows the regiment leaving Providence on April 20, 1861, to fight in the Civil War.

In 1933 Democrat Theodore F. Green was elected governor. During his term he pushed the legislature to pass bills providing for much-needed social programs.

Rhode Island was badly in need of some political changes. In 1932 Rhode Island elected a Democratic governor, Theodore Francis Green. Two years after Green was elected, the Democrats controlled both houses of Rhode Island's legislature. The day that the Democratic-controlled legislature was seated, Green assigned state troopers to guard the doors. He allowed no members to leave. Green wanted to make sure that they passed some badly needed state laws. In about half an hour, the legislature passed dozens of bills. They passed a bill limiting the work week to 48 hours. They provided for unemployment compensation, a minimum wage, and a retirement system. They fired the entire state Supreme Court and the state police commissioner as well. This became known as the "Bloodless Revolution."

The nation's economy stayed improved when the United States entered World War II late in 1941. American industries expanded and began manufacturing goods used in the war. Rhode Island factories produced ammunition and other war materials. The state's shipyards built cargo and military ships. In 1942, when thousands of men went to fight in the war, women went to work in the factories.

After the war unemployment rose again when factories stopped building war materials. By 1949 seventeen percent of the state's workers were out of jobs. Rhode Island undertook a massive effort to bring new and different kinds of industries into the state. It attracted companies that made electronic equipment, plastics, machinery, chemicals, health care products, and toys. By the 1970s Rhode Island's unemployment was down to three percent. An increase in tourism gave Rhode Island's economy another boost during the 1980s.

During the 1980s and 1990s, Rhode Island took steps to modernize its legislative and judicial system. In 1986 Rhode Island approved a new state constitution. It allows amendments to be added after it is approved by majority vote in both houses of the legislature and by a majority of the voters. In 1994 Rhode Island established a special court that only hears cases involving crimes with guns. Rhode Island's leaders have historically sought creative measures in the service of its citizens. These actions are part of that tradition.

A United States Navy submarine shares the water with recreational boaters off the coast of Newport.

Today's Providence is a blend of the old and the new. It is New England's third largest city and an important center of banking and commerce.

# The Fighting First Rhode Island

In 1774 about four thousand African Americans lived in Rhode Island. This number included both slaves and free people. Like other colonists African Americans were affected by the problems brought on by British rule. These problems included what the colonists considered unfair taxation and losses of property and liberty.

The situation in Rhode Island became tense in June 1774 when Great Britain made plans to close the port of Boston. This meant that goods could not be shipped out of Massachusetts. The Rhode Island Assembly worried that the British might close the harbor at Newport,

*This engraving depicts the Battle of Rhode Island in 1778. The First Rhode Island Regiment fought courageously against the invading British troops during this battle.*

too! Many men from Rhode Island signed up to serve in the Continental Army as well as in the state militia. Some free African Americans were part of these groups.

In July 1776, the Continental Congress declared independence on behalf of the 13 United States. In January 1777 General George Washington called for a regiment from Rhode Island. However, the tiny colony could not find enough men to create a regiment.

Brigadier-General James Mitchell Varnum had an idea. Why not recruit slaves? With General Washington's approval, the Rhode Island Assembly resolved that every able-bodied slave could enlist in the army. They would be entitled to the same wages and freedoms given to other soldiers. About 75 slaves joined the "First Rhode Island Regiment" in the first year.

The regiment's most important battle was the Battle of Rhode Island in August 1778. Its mission was to protect the right flank of the American forces. The regiment performed bravely, turning back wave after wave of British soldiers. The First Rhode Island served five more years. Not only did the regiment defend its home state, but it also participated in battles outside the colony, including the Battle of Yorktown, Virginia.

Throughout the war, officers commended the regiment for its bravery in battle and patience in desperate circumstances. After the war the First Rhode Island Regiment was dismissed. The African American soldiers were rewarded with something far more precious than medals or money, however. They were given their freedom.

# Changing with the Times

Rhode Island is the smallest state in the country. It covers just a little more than twelve hundred square miles. About sixty percent of that land is forested. Along the coastline are beaches and boat harbors. Farms—more than seven hundred of them—are scattered throughout the middle of the state.

Even though so much of its land is forests, farms, and seashore, Rhode Island is still the second most densely populated state. That means it has the second highest average number of people living in an area of a certain size. Rhode Island averages more than eight hundred people per square mile. More than three quarters of these people live within 15 miles of Providence, the state's manufacturing center.

Rhode Island produces about five billion dollars worth of manufactured goods a year. About twenty percent of the state's workers are employed in manufacturing. That's slightly higher than the national average. It's also one of the highest rates of manufacturing employment in any state. More than twenty percent of

These buildings are part of Providence's financial district. As an important financial center, Providence contributes greatly to the economy of the entire New England region.

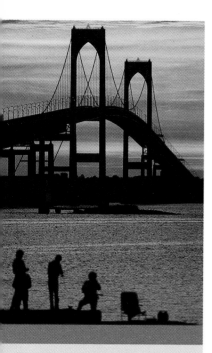

Newport Bridge over Narragansett Bay is one of the longest suspension bridges in the world. It cost $71 million to build. Its construction and maintenance has boosted Rhode Island's economy by providing jobs.

the total value of all goods and services produced in Rhode Island comes from manufacturing.

Jewelry and silverware are the state's most important areas of manufacturing. Included among the major products of this industry is jewelry made from precious metals, mostly gold and silver. The Trifari, Monet, Calibri, Allison Reed, and Sardelli jewelry companies all manufacture in Rhode Island. Less-expensive fashion jewelry, along with silver and silver-plated eating utensils and serving dishes, are also produced. The Gorham Silverware Company was the first silverware maker in the United States. It has been in business since 1818. Other items made in Rhode Island include crystal glass dishes and vases, award statues, and ballpoint pens. The A. T. Cross pen company is headquartered in Rhode Island.

Rhode Island's second most important manufacturing category is fabricated metal products. Rhode Island factories make nuts and bolts, wire, metal parts for machines, tools, and preformed metal items, such as pipe fittings. Scientific instruments, especially medical

The jewelry industry in the United States began in Providence. Jewelry manufacturing made Providence one of the most important industrial centers in New England by 1824.

and surgical instruments, are third in importance. Other products include electrical meters, navigation equipment, and weather instruments.

Rhode Island factories also produce electrical equipment for heating, air conditioning, and refrigeration. Nonelectric machinery, chemicals, textiles, and toys are also manufactured in the state. In fact Hasbro, one of the world's largest toymakers, is headquartered in Rhode Island.

As in all the states today, various kinds of service industries make up the largest category of Rhode Island's economy. About three quarters of the state's Gross State Product is derived from services of some kind. Service industries are those in which workers provide a service instead of make a product. Service employees may work at a retail store, a bank, a hospital, or a government agency. Rhode Island's service industries are centered around Providence.

First in importance are the financial, insurance, and real estate services. Providence is one of New England's most important banking centers. Two of its companies, Fleet Group and Citizens Bank, are large financial companies. The state's second largest area of service industries are community, social, and personal services. These include many of the kinds of businesses people deal with every day. Some of them are law firms, doctors' offices and private hospitals, architectural and computer programming companies, and repair shops.

Wholesale and retail trade is the third largest Rhode Island service industry. Wholesale trade takes place when one business sells goods to another

The United States Navy is the largest single employer in Newport County. It is second only to the state government as the largest employer in Rhode Island.

A large part of Rhode Island's farm income comes from milk produced on dairy farms such as this one.

business for resale. Retail trade consists of selling items directly to individuals. For example, an auto parts factory selling to an auto parts store is wholesale trade. When that store sells to individual car owners, retail trade takes place.

The fourth-ranking service industry in Rhode Island is government services. Public schools, public hospitals, and government offices make up a large part of this category. Military bases are also very important. Newport has a large naval base. During World War II, Rhode Island was a training center for aircraft carrier pilots and naval construction forces that built bridges and airfields. Today, Newport is home to the Naval Education and Training Center. It also houses under-water-training centers and a naval-training center for officers.

The load of lumber on this freighter's deck will be transported like many other Rhode Island prod-ucts—by boat.

A final area of Rhode Island's service industry is transportation, communication, and utilities. Several large shipping and trucking companies are headquartered in the state.

Rhode Island has been a place for vacations since before the Civil War. Miles of beach and shoreline along Narragansett Bay and the Atlantic Ocean draw hundreds of thousands of tourists to Rhode Island every year. In fact tourism is one of Rhode Island's most important industries. From the early 1980s to the mid-1990s, tourist revenue more than doubled. Today, it totals nearly $1.7 billion a year.

Agriculture plays a small role in Rhode Island's economy. It accounts for only about one percent of the total value of all goods and services produced in the state. About two thirds of Rhode Island's agricultural income comes from greenhouses and nurseries. They produce sod, ornamental trees and shrubs, Christmas trees, and flowering plants. Milk and other dairy products are also important agricultural products.

The state's fishing industry brings in about $85 million a year. Flounder is the most abundant catch, followed by cod, tuna, and whiting. Clams, lobsters, and scallops are also found in Rhode Island waters.

Rhode Island was once known strictly for its manufacturing. It has taken many decades for the state to develop the variety of industries that make up today's economy. This variety is important because it assures that the economy will continue to be strong even if certain industries decline.

These fishing boats are docked at Point Judith in Narragansett Bay. The fish catch in Rhode Island has declined in recent years, but fishing is still a significant source of income.

Sailing on Newport Bay is one of the activities that draws thousands of tourists to Rhode Island each year.

# A Woman with Choices

Many people Diane Worthen grew up with work in Rhode Island's factories or textile mills. "I understand that people have to work in the mills," she says. "That's their survival. But it's too locked in for me. I could never do that kind of work."

For many years people living in Rhode Island have worked in mills and jewelry factories. It was accepted the same way as the people of Tennessee accepted working in the mines, or the people of Alabama accepted working in the cotton fields. Most of them didn't have any choice. Many of them still don't. But Diane Worthen knew she had to break away.

"I was brought up in a large family of nine children. If you wanted something, you had to get it yourself. Nobody was going to give you anything. I think that's where I got the idea that I could get the life I wanted by working hard. I knew nothing would be handed to me, so I was willing to work for it."

That willingness to work hard has kept Rhode Island's mills running for nearly two centuries. But Diane came along at a different point in history. She became a carpenter working in construction. A woman couldn't have gotten that job a generation ago. But Diane did, and she loved it. She liked being outside. She liked making things. She liked having a choice.

At first some of the male carpenters resented her being on the job. "It was tough when I first began," she says. "But once they saw that I knew what I was doing, they began to respect me. Some of them even started asking me questions. I think that, no matter what job you have, you encounter fences you have to climb."

During the last ten years of the thirteen she worked as a carpenter, Diane attended night school at the Rhode Island School of Design. She specialized in lighting design. Now she has a new job as manager of a lighting showroom. "Contractors come to me needing solutions to their lighting problems," she says. "I assist them in drawing blueprints that include the wiring and lighting for their buildings."

Diane feels good that she's still working in the building industry and using the skills she learned in school. "The only thing I don't like about this job," she says with a grin, "is that I don't get outside often enough."

She says that, "Nowadays, we have more of a choice than ever before. Women don't have to get married at nineteen or twenty and raise a family. They can wait a little longer and then decide how many children they want to have." Diane did wait until she met the right man. Today, she's married with a baby girl. But she has her career, too. Both she and her husband agree that being a mother will not make her give that up. For the time being, she can have the best of both worlds.

*Diane Worthen worked as a carpenter for 13 years, but now she advises builders about interior lighting.*

*Downtown Providence has seen a great deal of new construction during the past several decades.*

29

# Centuries of Contributions

For a small state, Rhode Island has produced a remarkable number of artists who have made an impact on this country. From writers to designers, from performing artists to painters, Rhode Island artists have inspired us and cheered us.

Perhaps the most familiar work of art by a Rhode Islander is a song that has played an important role in American history. Julia Ward Howe was a nineteenth-century poet and writer. She worked all her life to abolish slavery and achieve rights for women. At the time of the Civil War, she wrote verses to accompany a popular marching tune. The result was "The Battle Hymn of the Republic." Howe was also the first woman elected to the American Academy of Arts and Letters in 1908.

Around the turn of the century, another Rhode Islander began to write songs and musical shows. For decades George M. Cohan wrote, produced, and starred in the most popular musicals on Broadway. He created more than forty shows. His most popular songs

This is Brown University's Carrie Tower. Brown is an Ivy League university and one of the oldest colleges in the United States.

include "You're a Grand Old Flag," "Yankee Doodle Dandy," "Give My Regards to Broadway," and "Over There," a patriotic World War I song.

Providence has also nurtured many fine writers. Edwin O'Connor won the 1962 Pulitzer Prize for *The Edge of Sadness*, his novel about three generations of an American family. One of Providence's most original writers is enjoying a surge of popularity today, almost sixty years after his death. H. P. Lovecraft wrote primarily for the magazine *Weird Tales* during the twenty years before his death in 1937. His works were forgotten for nearly four decades. Then, in the 1970s, some of his fantasy and horror stories were published in paperback. He wrote of supernatural beings and bizarre experiments. Many of his chilling tales have been made into movies.

Most people carry a portrait by Rhode Island's most famous painter in their pockets every day. Gilbert Stuart was the colonies' principal artist during the late

The Breakers, a seventy-room mansion, was built in 1895 for multimillionaire Cornelius Vanderbilt II. It is one of the grand houses in Newport that is now open to tourists.

1700s and early 1800s. He painted portraits of several United States Presidents. Stuart's portrait of George Washington is one of the best-known paintings ever done by an American artist. That portrait is the one used on the one-dollar bill!

There are few states that can match Rhode Island for historical sites. Rhode Islanders value their history, and they are serious about preserving it. One of Rhode Island's most famous historical sites is Slater Mill, next to the Blackstone River in Pawtucket. This was the very first spinning mill in the nation. In addition Providence has dozens of restored homes from the last half of the eighteenth century. The John Brown House, built in 1786, has been called the nation's "most magnificent and elegant private mansion." Newport has more than three hundred buildings from colonial times. One of these is Hunter House, built in 1748. It served as the command headquarters for the French Navy that helped the colonies during the Revolutionary War.

Because it was the first colony to offer religious freedom, Rhode Island has some of the oldest churches in the nation. Also, the Touro Synagogue National Historical Site in Newport houses North America's oldest Jewish synagogue, dedicated in 1763. Newport also has one of the nation's oldest Quaker meeting-houses, part of which was built in 1699, and the oldest Seventh Day Adventist Baptist meetinghouse, built in 1729. Providence is the home of the nation's oldest Baptist church. It was begun by the town's founder Roger Williams in 1638. The church building was built in 1775.

The Beechwood Mansion in Newport was built in 1856 for the Astor family.

Costumed actors re-create life as it was during the 1890s at Rhode Island's Beechwood Mansion.

One interesting thing about many of Rhode Island's historic buildings is that they're still in use. Some of the churches still hold services. In Providence and Newport, there are hundreds of private residences that have been lived in continuously since before the Revolutionary War. Near Little Compton in southeastern Rhode Island, Gray's Store has been selling food and candy since 1788. Brown & Hopkins Country Store in Chepachet is the nation's oldest continuously operating general store. It has sold food, hardware, farm implements, and furniture since 1809.

Along the seacoast of Newport, in the late 1800s, some of the richest families in America built homes. Some of them were modeled after historic European villas. Inside, they contain gilded carvings, classical paintings, and fine furniture.

In addition to the art displayed in its famous buildings, Rhode Island has several notable art museums. The Rhode Island School of Design's Museum of Art in Providence shows furnishings as well as paintings and sculpture. Brown University's Bell Gallery, also in Providence, hosts traveling exhibitions and works by local artists.

Rhode Island also supports the performing arts. The Tony Award-winning Trinity Square Repertory Company is a theater that was started in 1964 in Providence. People donated their time to build sets, make costumes, and perform in the plays. Now they have a regular audience, and Trinity Square produces award-winning plays. Another theater company, the Providence Players, is the oldest community theater in the United States.

The JVC Jazz Festival in Newport presents extraordinary musicians from all over the world. It is the most famous event of its kind in the country. For those who love folk music, the Newport Folk Festival provides the same high-quality entertainment.

Rhode Island's culture, although steeped in history, has a message for today: Any piece of work, whether it is a mansion or a moment on the stage, can endure for centuries. All it takes is the ability of the artist to express himself or herself uniquely from within.

The Rhode Island School of Design is considered one of the best art schools in the world. It combines professional training in art and design with a traditional college education.

# Magical Memories

Today, most people call them "merry-go-rounds." But in the heyday of amusement parks, from 1880 through the 1930s, they were called carousels. For the last century, children, grandparents, and families have loved carousels. There was—and is—something almost magical about the handsome horses, the colorful saddles, and the distinctive organ music.

In the last decades of the nineteenth century, carousels were also works of art. The horses were hand-carved from solid oak. Then they were painted by hand. One of the most skillful carousel makers was Charles I. D. Looff, a woodcarver from Denmark. He came to America in 1870, at the age of 18. Within ten years his carousels were featured in amusement parks up and down the East Coast. He settled in Rhode Island. Eventually the small state had more than a dozen of his carousels. Four were at Crescent Park in East Providence.

But the years were not kind to carousels or to the amusement parks

*The restored Crescent Park carousel brings back the fun and magic of a bygone era.*

that housed them. As they fell out of fashion, the gilt paint on the carousel horses wore away. The wood dried, then cracked and split. Often entire carousels were demolished and sold as scrap, or the horses were sold one by one to collectors.

The people of East Providence were determined that these fates would not befall the one remaining Crescent Park carousel. In 1978 voters overwhelmingly decided to buy the carousel and its land for a half-million dollars. Then the citizens of East Providence got busy. They came with hammers, sandpaper, and paintbrushes to clean the framework of the carousel, and they hired professionals to restore the carousel horses.

Today, the carousel in Crescent Park in East Providence is almost fully restored to its original condition. It took a lot of memories—and a lot of hard work—to bring the magic back. But the people who come to Crescent Park are happy the carousel is running again.

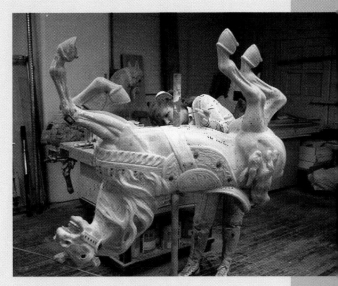

*East Providence residents hired professional restorers to repair the Crescent Park carousel. Here, a repaired and sanded horse is ready to be painted.*

*From about 1880 to 1910, Charles I. D. Looff, shown here with his wife, was the undisputed king of carousel construction.*

37

# Jazzing It Up in Newport

For most of the year, the seaside resort town of Newport, Rhode Island, seems like any other small town in the United States. But every August Newport comes alive with the exciting sounds of jazz. The reason is the JVC Jazz Festival, and the sounds are created by some of the best jazz musicians in the world. The jazz comes in all styles: acoustic, electric, brassy, vocalized, free-form, and melodic. Newport's jazz festival was the first such music festival in the United States.

The Newport Jazz Festival was originally the idea of a wealthy young Newport couple, Mr. and Mrs. Louis Lorillard. They formed a corporation called Newport Jazz Festival, Inc. The corporation's mission was "to encour-

*Wynton Marsalis, one of the world's premiere jazz trumpet players, performs at the JVC Jazz Festival.*

*Improvisation is one of the most distinctive elements in jazz music. Players often make up the music as they go along—which means they have to make it sound good the first time.*

age America's enjoyment of jazz . . . our country's only original art form." The Lorillards' dream was to bring world-class jazz musicians together in Newport for an American jazz festival.

The Lorillards invited some of their friends to help pay for the event. The year was 1954, and although jazz was a popular musical form, few of the Lorillards' friends were familiar with jazz music. When all but two friends refused, the Lorillards hosted the festival by themselves. They solicited sponsors from the music world, including world-famous composer and conductor Leonard Bernstein. They hired music producer George Wein to handle the details.

The Lorillards employed some of the biggest names in jazz music to perform at the festival—performers whose music eventually shaped jazz history. Among the first festival musicians were Chicago-style clarinetist Pee Wee Russell, drummer Gene Krupa, and guitarist Eddie Condon. Swing vocalists Ella Fitzgerald and Billie Holiday were there, as were band leaders Stan Kenton and Oscar Peterson. The father of bebop, trumpeter Dizzy Gillespie, and cool jazz saxophonists Lee Konitz and Gerry

Mulligan thrilled the crowd with their original sounds. About 65 musicians from all over the country performed music that ranged from rollicking, brassy Dixieland jazz to cool, mellow, modern jazz.

The first Newport Jazz Festival was presented on the outdoor grass tennis courts of the International Tennis Hall of Fame. Because many people had never heard jazz music before, the festival included lectures on the history of jazz. Between sets band leader Stan Kenton explained the different types of jazz to the audience.

For the Lorillards hosting the festival was an act of faith. The festival cost more than $40,000. If nobody had attended, the Lorillards would have lost all that money. Instead, more than 14,000 people came, twice as many as were expected, and the new corporation made an $11,000 profit.

Before the first concert was over, the Lorillards and George Wein knew they were going to hold the festival again the following year. The Newport Jazz Festival became an annual event. At its peak in the mid-1960s, yearly attendance topped fifty thousand.

Today, Newport's jazz festival is still going strong. In fact it has become internationally known, with performances given each year by jazz greats such as Al Di Meola, Jean-Luc Ponty, Grover Washington, Jr., and Gerry Mulligan. George Wein, still producing the festival after more than forty years, has become a familiar name to jazz fans.

*The JVC Jazz Festival provides all of the excitement and fun of live performance.*

*Some people arrive at the JVC Jazz Festival by boat.*

A few things have changed since that first festival. For more than a decade, the festival has been sponsored by JVC, a manufacturer of audio and video equipment. The annual event is now called the JVC Jazz Festival. The first concert of each year's festival is still performed on the courts of the International Tennis Hall of Fame. The remainder of the jazz festival, however, takes place about a mile up the road at Fort Adams State Park. Fort Adams is a Civil War fort that looks out at Narragansett Bay. Grass stretches from the walls of the fort all the way to the bay. There, thousands of jazz lovers thrill to the sounds of their favorite musicians while enjoying cool ocean breezes.

The success of Newport's festival has motivated other cities around the country to host their own jazz festivals. Today, jazz festivals are held every year in Monterey, Chicago, New Orleans, and New York City. Festivals are also held in France, Switzerland, Poland, Germany, and many other countries. What started out as the Lorillards' dream has become a tradition in the world of music.

# Harboring the Future

Rhode Islanders are determined to create an economy that will remain healthy into the twenty-first century. From the mid-1980s through the mid-1990s, employment rose in every area but one. The state lost more than 25,000 manufacturing jobs. The overall trend is positive, however, and the state is looking for ways to create new jobs while preventing the further loss of current ones.

In Providence, people are excited about the new jobs that came with the completion of the Capital Center Project. The goal of this project was to develop and expand the Capital Center district in downtown Providence. The people who developed the plan were dedicated to preserving Providence's colonial charm. None of the older buildings were torn down, although some were restored. The project expanded the Capital Center by about 77 acres. More importantly it brought thousands of new jobs to the area. Included in the project were brand-new office buildings, hotels, and shops.

An issue of even greater concern is the environ-

Block Island's Mohegan Bluffs rise two hundred feet above the ocean and stretch for three miles. The preservation of natural areas is one of the challenges facing Rhode Island in the future.

Coastal communities, such as Wickford, will benefit greatly from the cleanup of Narragansett Bay.

mental decline of Narragansett Bay. Rhode Island has established antipollution and cleanup systems for the bay. The sewage treatment plants that were built in the late 1800s were no longer effective. After a heavy rainfall, the storm water sometimes filled the treatment plants. When this happened, both storm water and sewage poured untreated into the bay. Narragansett Bay is important to everyone from commercial fishers to sailboaters. The fishing industry in Rhode Island is worth about $85 million a year, and many jobs depend on keeping the bay clean. This issue is now being addressed by the Narrangansett Bay Project, and Rhode Island now has some of the strictest antipollution laws in the nation.

Currently the Save the Bay organization conducts educational workshops and protest demonstrations. Its members also bring polluters to court. Their goal is for cities and towns to build adequate water-treatment facilities.

The best of Rhode Island is still to come. A renewed Narragansett Bay and Capital Center will improve the quality of life for many Rhode Islanders. These achievements will also help them to imagine what else can be done to shape the ideal future of Rhode Island.

# Important Historical Events

**1524** Giovanni da Verrazano explores present-day Rhode Island.

**1614** Dutch navigator Adriaen Block sails past the Rhode Island coast and names Block Island after himself.

**1636** Roger Williams flees Massachusetts Bay Colony and founds Providence.

**1638** Anne Hutchinson, William Coddington, and John Clarke found Pocasset, now Portsmouth.

**1639** Coddington and Clarke leave Pocasset and found Newport.

**1643** Samuel Gorton founds Warwick.

**1644** Roger Williams receives a charter for Rhode Island from Parliament.

**1647** The four settlements in Rhode Island form a loose confederation under the Williams charter.

**1663** A second charter is granted, which will remain Rhode Island law for 180 years.

**1675** King Philip's War begins.

**1676** Metacomet is killed near Mount Hope, now Bristol.

**1769** Newport citizens burn the British customs ship *Liberty*.

**1772** Providence citizens board the British warship *Gaspee*. They shoot and wound the captain and burn the ship.

**1774** Rhode Island prohibits bringing slaves into the colony.

**1776** On May 4 Rhode Island is the first colony to declare its independence from Great Britain.

**1784** A state emancipation act frees all Rhode Island slaves.

**1790** Rhode Island approves the United States Constitution on May 29, after insisting on the inclusion of the Bill of Rights. It thus becomes the thirteenth state.

**1793** The first water-powered spinning machine is built in Pawtucket.

**1842** Thomas Dorr leads a revolt against the state government. He fails, but a new state constitution is accepted.

**1895** A new breed of chicken, the Rhode Island Red, is officially recognized.

**1935** Governor Theodore Francis Green and fellow Democrats control the state legislature and pass badly needed modernization laws in the "Bloodless Revolution."

**1938** A hurricane kills 258 people and destroys one hundred million dollars worth of property.

**1954** The first United States jazz festival is held in Newport.

**1969** The Newport Bridge between Newport and Jamestown is completed.

**1971** A personal income tax is passed by the state legislature.

**1991** After 259 years of ownership, the Crandall family of Westerly, who could no longer maintain the land, returns hundreds of acres to the Narragansett.

**1998** Rhode Island and other states file suit against the Environmental Protection Agency to establish ozone controls on Midwest power plants.

The flag of Rhode Island is white, commemorating the Rhode Islanders who lost their lives in the Revolutionary War. It has a gold anchor in the center, representing hope. It is surrounded by 13 gold stars, symbolizing the original colonies. Beneath the anchor is a blue banner bearing the state motto: "Hope." By state law the flag must be edged by gold fringe, and the flagpole must be topped by a spearhead.

# Rhode Island Almanac

**Nickname.** The Ocean State

**Capital.** Providence

**State Bird.** Rhode Island Red

**State Flower.** Violet

**State Tree.** Red maple

**State Motto.** Hope

**State Song.** "Rhode Island"

**State Abbreviations.** R.I. (traditional); RI (postal)

**Statehood.** May 29, 1790, the 13th state

**Government.** Congress: U.S. senators, 2; U.S. representatives, 2. State Legislature: senators, 50; representatives, 100. Counties: 5, but no county governments. State is governed by 39 municipalities

**Area.** 1,213 sq mi (3,142 sq km), 50th in size among the states

**Greatest Distances.** north/south, 59 mi (95 km); east/west, 40 mi (64 km). Coastline: 40 mi (65 km)

**Elevation.** Highest: Jerimoth Hill, 812 ft (247 m). Lowest: sea level, along the Atlantic Ocean

**Population.** 1990 Census: 1,005,984 (6% increase from 1980), 43rd among the states. Density: 829 persons per sq mi (320 persons per sq km). Distribution: 87% urban, 13% rural. 1980 Census: 947,154

**Economy.** *Agriculture:* greenhouse and nursery products, milk, dairy products, Christmas trees, potatoes, hay, apples, vegetables, chickens, turkeys. *Fishing:* flounder, lobsters, clams, cod, tuna, whiting, scallops. *Manufacturing:* jewelry, silverware, fabricated metal products, scientific instruments, heating, air conditioning, and refrigeration equipment, nonelectrical machinery, chemicals, textiles, toys. *Mining:* sand and gravel, stone

*State Seal*

*State Flower:* Violet

*State Bird:* Rhode Island Red

# Annual Events

★ Rhode Island Heritage Month, statewide (May)

★ Festival of Historic Houses in Providence (June)

★ Bristol Fourth of July Parade— oldest in America

★ Classical Music Festival in Newport (July)

★ Hall of Fame Tennis Championships in Newport (July)

★ Folk Music Festival in Newport (August)

★ Jazz Festival in Newport (August)

★ Narragansett Powwow in Charlestown (August)

★ State Fair in Richmond (August)

★ Christmas in Newport (December)

# Places to Visit

★ Benefit Street's "Mile of History" colonial homes in Providence

★ The Breakers mansion in Newport

★ Cliff Walk in Newport

★ Crescent Park Carousel in East Providence

★ First Baptist Church in America in Providence

★ General Nathanael Greene Homestead in Coventry

★ Gilbert Stuart Birthplace in Saunderstown

★ International Tennis Hall of Fame in Newport

★ John Brown House in Providence

★ Marble House in Newport

★ Old Stone Mill in Newport

★ Rhode Island School of Design Art Museum in Providence

★ Slater Mill Historic Site in Pawtucket

# Index